GENERATIONS OF LOVE

Rosary Meditations for Grandparents

Anne M. Belle-Oudry

Caritas Press, USA

GENERATIONS OF LOVE
Rosary Meditations for Grandparents

Anne M. Belle-Oudry

First Edition

10 9 8 7 6 5 4 3 2 1

ISBN 978-1-940209-01-2

For reorders:
LilyTrilogy.com
CatholicWord.com
Sherry@LilyTrilogy.com

Published by Caritas Press, Arizona, USA

All for the Glory of God!

To my husband, Jack; my daughters, Jaclene, Jillian and Grace; my sons-in-law, Nick and Jake; and my grandson, Austin David Jack. You all bring me closer to the heart of God. I love you more than words can say.

And to my heroes: my parents, Mary Ellen Beattie DeMato and Joseph Michael DeMato; my grandparents, Nanny (Katherine Duffy Beattie), Foggy (George Wilson Beattie), Nana Roni (Alvenia DeMato Schiavone), and Grandpa John (John Schiavone). I love you all so much. Thank you for your sacrifices, your tender love and for sharing your wisdom with me. Pray for me as I pray for you.

INTRODUCTION

One spring afternoon, long ago, my brothers and sisters ran toward the screen door. They were on their way to the front yard to play kickball. By choice, I was last in line. Not being the most athletic of the eight, I didn't mind falling behind these talented stars. As they passed the living room couch, each in turn whispered, "Hi Nanny" to our beautiful Irish grandmother. Nanny and Foggy (My oldest brother could not say "grandfather," and the name stuck) were wonderful role models, loving and caring frequent visitors from New York City to our farmhouse on Long Island.

When it was my turn to greet Nanny and run through the door, a glistening object caught my eye. Nanny was holding her Rosary beads. I slowed down, and before I realized it, I had stopped and was staring at the beads that seemed almost to be glowing, slipping one by one through her delicate fingers. I was mesmerized.

Without looking up, Nanny tapped the couch and motioned me to sit down, and I got my first lesson in the Most Holy Rosary, as Nanny Beattie led me through the wonderful mysteries of Jesus' life. I am forever grateful to my mother's mother for giving me the gift that has helped me know Jesus, peace and love.

It's hard to believe so much time has passed, but that little girl, who, by the way, never did join her siblings in that kickball game, is now a grandmother with a whole new appreciation for the power of prayer. What could be a better use of our time than praying for our families? God can help them more than we can. We can pray that God assists them during difficult moments and have confidence He will hear us. We can offer our prayers to help our children and grandchildren grow in love. We can ask God for the grace to love them unconditionally.

I have seen firsthand how a prayerful person can inspire others to pray, even with just a little pat on the couch cushion. That invitation from Nanny has turned into a deep devotion to the Rosary, one of the most powerful tools we have in this often uncertain and sometimes difficult world. Nanny proved something that day, and I would like to prove it as well: grandparents can be a powerful link between God and their grandchildren.

St. Joachim and St. Anne, grandparents of Jesus, pray for us. Blessed Mother, pray for us as we seek to do God's will. Help us remember that God's will is always to love. St. Joseph, protector, watch over us.

THE JOYFUL MYSTERIES

1

THE ANNUNCIATION

"Hail, Full of Grace, the Lord is with you!"
Luke 1:28

I imagine that when the Angel Gabriel appeared to Mary, she was praying to God the Father. Hearing the greeting "full of grace" really would have perplexed her. She was very humble. "Full of grace" means completely containing the life of God. Completely? That is something to ponder. That would mean she had been given all of the gifts of the Holy Spirit. That title had to help move Mary to want to do God's will. Knowing that she was very small, she would put all her trust in God to be what He wanted her to be. Her humility would tell her that, on her own, she could not do such a great task. But being "full of grace" meant that she had the fullness of God's life within her, so He would be her help in every need.

When the angel exclaimed, "The Lord is with you," he was telling Mary of God the Father's eternal plan for her. She knew Sacred Scripture well. She knew the ancient prophecies of the Virgin bearing the Savior.

She understood that our Lord and Savior would take shape within her.

I remember the moment when I first learned I would be blessed with a child. There is no other moment in life quite like that one. Immediately I felt my heart grow. I had a new purpose, a new perspective on perfect beauty, perfect love and perfect sacrifice. And then twenty-six years later, I experienced a whole new kind of joy when that daughter told me she now carried a blessing within her womb.

After looking at the tiny figure in the ultrasound photo, everything changed. *I am a grandmother!* No need to wait nine months to celebrate this fact. I could plainly (well, almost plainly) see my precious grandchild. Boy or girl, brunette or blond - it didn't matter. This wonderful gift from God is my grandchild, forever, for all eternity! Let the celebrations begin! Love multiplies in the most beautiful way.

Thank You, Jesus, for the gift of grandchildren. Through this cherished gift, You bring me to a closer understanding of how You love us. Is it possible that we bring the same delight to Your heart that our adorable, irresistible grandchildren bring to ours?

Help me, Jesus, to teach my grandchildren You are with us with infinite love. With little eyes watching me, I want to strive all the more to reflect Your perfect love and do as Mary did, proclaiming "Behold I am the handmaid of the Lord."

With each "Hail Mary" increase in me the desire to say, "Yes!" to You, Lord.

2.

THE VISITATION

"In those days Mary arose and went with haste into the hill country, to a city of Judah ... and greeted Elizabeth." Luke 1:39

I can imagine the joy Elizabeth felt when she saw the familiar, friendly face of her cousin willing to lend a hand. How soothing Mary's sweet, gentle kindness and her holy presence must have been at that wonderful time in Elizabeth's life, when she was preparing for her newborn son.

Some of the most joyous times of my life have been visits from family members, especially my grandparents. The moment I saw their car parked under our massive oak tree, a celebration would start in my heart. I loved talking, listening and laughing with them. I loved walking, singing and just being together. I loved eating pie with them and just sitting admiring them. They always dressed nicely—Nanny in her pretty dresses with her hair curled and Foggy in His handsome suit and that wonderful fedora. I loved seeing Nana Roni, (we couldn't pronounce "Schiavone") the one person who always brought me stories of my fabulous Daddy. I loved feeling connected to the past as they shared memories with me.

And now, I get to be that special person in someone's life. Immediately after my new grandbaby's birth, my husband and I had the privilege of visiting. How adorable! We were filled with gladness for our daughter and son-in-law. Already they were such good parents. It was a time of work and exhaustion, rest and reflection. Here we were, two generations working to care for the next.

I felt great love, like we were being visited by God through this baby. When my daughter's mother-in-law, Catherine, arrived, it gave us a beautiful opportunity as one big loving family to welcome this child, each of us bringing our ancestors along. We shared hopes and dreams of happiness and health. We talked about precious baby sounds and little faces seeming to take after one or another of us. We talked about chins and noses and hair. It's funny how these things help us connect. We bonded as one big unit. All of us ready to love and care for this little baby. There to do whatever was asked of us.

Jesus, I know what I am feeling is Your love flowing through me. May I always feel this close to You and all those You put in my life, so that I may share Your love with everyone. Help us remember what a great gift it is to our grandchildren that we love each other—immediate family and extended family. May love and service be our mission, just as it was Mary's on her visit to her cousin Elizabeth.

3.

THE NATIVITY

"You will find an infant wrapped in swaddling clothes and lying in a manger."   Luke 2:12

Jesus, we kneel before You, our awesome God as a newborn baby, born into the world to live among us, show us the way and lay down Your life for us. Born into poverty, You remind us not to spoil our family with material things. You show us Your love for the poor by choosing to be born poor.

Jesus, help me to live simply as my grandparents did. They taught me that, to love, you do not need to have many possessions. They gave their time, showing me what is really important in life.

This past Christmas, my youngest daughter had a little clay Nativity on her dresser. Every afternoon, we would look at it with Austin, my grandson. As we told him who everyone was, he always wanted to kiss Jesus and Our Blessed Mother. Pointing out the Three Wise Men, we would sing over and over, "We three Kings of Orient are, bearing gifts we traverse afar."

Sometime later, Austin kept repeating, "we we we." Finally we realized he wanted to "visit" the Nativity set. He got so excited to see and greet all the holy people and little animals. As the days went by, he began saying "we we we" if he saw the three wise men in a book, or when he recognized their silhouettes on a Christmas card. Just fourteen months old at the time, this little guy had such understanding and recognition. When we heard the "Three Wise Men" were going to be at the zoo for a Christmas celebration, we knew we had to take him to meet them in person. He was in awe.

May we all have that kind of awe, Jesus, when we contemplate the nativity and meditate on Your humility and the greatness of Your love. May we remember that adoring You in the manger is much like adoring You in the Eucharist. We love and adore that beautiful baby come to save us. We adore the Eucharist, loving us, giving us Your very life. No one partakes of the Eucharist before adoring and kneeling in thanksgiving, not even the priest.

May we always treasure the time we have with our Lord in the most Blessed Sacrament and the time we have together loving each other and leading each other closer to Christ.

4.

THE PRESENTATION

"And when the time came for their purification according to the law of Moses, they brought Him up to Jerusalem to present Him to the Lord."
Luke 2:22

Mary and Joseph knew who Jesus was: the Son of God, the Messiah. Mary could have said, "We don't need to go through this ritual of purification. This baby is the King of the Universe, and I am His Mother!" But she did not do that. Following the laws God gave to Moses, Joseph and Mary brought Jesus to the Temple. They went out of love and faithful obedience to God.

They knew that God loves us and that we need to respond to His love. Faith, love and obedience are all connected. We cannot love without faith and obedience. Jesus said, "I did not come to do my will but the will of the one who sent me."

Nanny would ask my mother with the birth of each child, "When is the baptism?" She felt the most important way to be obedient to God's commands was to have a new baby baptized as soon as possible. She would always say nothing is as important as baptism. Years later, when my mom, aunts

15

and uncles visited Ireland, the place of Nanny's birth, they discovered that the birthdate we all knew for her, the day we celebrated as her birthday, was actually the day she was baptized!

Obedience that springs from love draws us closer to God. We come to know Him when we obey His will and do what He wants us to do.

If we believe and have faith in all that God has said, we will obey. In obeying, we choose to live good lives. In living well, we are purified in our hearts. With pure hearts and by God's grace, we are given the gift of understanding our faith. Being obedient takes the pressure off us and frees us to love. Immediately deciding to do whatever is required of us simply makes everything easier.

God the Father, give me perfect obedience so that I can love You more. I want to be close to You in all things. I want to be face to face with You for eternity. Purify my heart. Help me model to my family great obedience to Your will so that they will want to love and follow You too.

5

FINDING JESUS IN THE TEMPLE

"And all who heard Him were amazed at His understanding and His answers."
Luke 2:47

Oh Jesus, what a beautiful sight! A perfect little boy of twelve, sitting among the elders and the teachers, talking about Scripture. If I place myself there, I want to ask You so many questions. I yearn to hear Your responses. I want to see the love You have for the Father written on Your adorable face. I want to spend time with You, Jesus, talking and listening to You.

Meditating on the gospel is my special time with the Lord. Finding Him in Scripture gives me opportunities to listen, feel His love and grow closer to Him.

When I was young, Foggy told me he had read the entire Bible many times. Touched by this, I imagined if my grandfather could do it, maybe I could too. Praying that God would help me read better, I wanted to be a great person like Foggy someday.

He was funny and outgoing, prone to humorous quips. He had charisma. Foggy would arrive at a park and in two minutes make new friends. He talked, laughed, listened and offered us Chiclets, during our long walks with their pampered dog, Duffy. He loved to sing and even crafted his own violin and taught himself to play.

I think back on the many ways Foggy helped us to "find" Jesus. In my early childhood, Foggy was a New York City bus driver. When I was four years old and my darling twin sisters, Jean and Joan, were three, mom would take us onboard his bus and we would sing our made-up jingles to the other passengers. Foggy loved it! So when he and Nanny visited, we sang all kinds of wonderful songs together under the towering pines in our backyard. His love made me feel so close to my sisters. We could be bickering one minute, full of joy the next. We found Jesus in that love for each other, inspired by the love Foggy had for all of us.

Our generations coming together give us a history we can draw from, as we grow into a strong forgiving family. We belong to our family and we belong to God.

We find You, Jesus, in the love and charity we share. Help us to be a holy family that loves unconditionally, overlooks each other's faults and finds You among us.

THE
LUMINOUS
MYSTERIES

1.

THE BAPTISM OF JESUS

"In those days Jesus came from Nazareth of Galilee and was baptized by John in the Jordan. And when He came out of the water, immediately He saw the heavens opened and the Spirit descending upon Him like a dove; and a voice came from heaven, 'You are my beloved Son; with You I am well pleased.'"

Mark 1:9-11

When Jesus approached John the Baptist, He got in line right behind sinners. He, who was sinless, who will baptize us in the Holy Spirit, humbly showed us the way.

I was there when my grandson, Austin, came to the church with a human life, and during Baptism, a supernatural life was bestowed on his soul. He came with his human parents, and after Baptism, also had heavenly parentage. I understood the eternity in Austin's baptism more than I ever comprehended with my own children. I remember wanting to baptize my girls right away as Nanny had always said to do. And I remember feeling joy that their original sin was washed away and they were welcomed into the Church. A great day! But when Austin was baptized, a clearer and deeper understanding surfaced in my heart, a knowledge that he had become a child of God, and a temple of the Holy Spirit and that his supernatural life had begun. I wasn't present for his physical birth but I witnessed his supernatural birth. He indeed had been born again as the Holy Spirit entered his soul, washed away his original sin and gave him God's very life. I was filled with inexpressible joy! How can I describe the gratitude I feel to God for allowing me to be present at such a miraculous event? How can I thank Him for showing me my faith lives on? Faith is the greatest gift to my children and my children's children. Witnessing it is my greatest joy.

"You are my beloved Son." Those are the words God the Father spoke at the baptism of Jesus. Did Jesus' heart race with joy when His Father called Him "beloved?" When I was baptized, did God the Father call me beloved? I became a child of God, a new creation, who can call God "Father." And so did all my loved ones who have received this unfathomable gift.

Jesus taught us to dare to call God "Abba," which means daddy. It was wrong in biblical times, and still is in some places today, to call the Creator of the Universe "Father." There is a fear that doing so will imply that humans are of the same nature as God. But Jesus taught us that God the Father wants a close, intimate, loving relationship with us; not one of master and servant, but one of parent and child. May we be forever grateful for the enormous gift of baptism. God grant us the grace to understand this amazing treasure!

2.

THE WEDDING FEAST AT CANA

"When the wine ran short, the mother of Jesus said to Him, 'They have no wine.' And Jesus said to her, 'Woman, how does your concern affect me? My hour has not yet come.' His mother said to the servers, 'Do whatever He tells you.'"   John 2:3-5

With loving concern, Holy Mother Mary noticed the wedding couple's plight and told Jesus about it. She didn't ask anything of Him. She did not say to "fix it" or give instructions on how to proceed. She simply trusted that He would respond to her intercession. She had faith in Him.

How many times have I told God of a problem or need, asked for His help and then told Him how to fix it? My Blessed Mother Mary is a wonderful example of loving God's will and not my own. She trusts God, in her beautiful humility, knowing His will is perfect love and mercy.

Nanny knew that too and tenderly trusted in that mercy. That fact might have gone unnoticed by some, but I came to understand it because I watched her closely, as grandchildren often do.

Nanny intrigued me. I'd seen her bow her head in prayer, and I'd seen her sit on the edge of her seat in front of the TV, punching the air to root on her favorite wrestler. She spoke eloquently of Jesus and could also yell out a window to my brothers below, instructing them how to win a fight. She could be strict, but melt in sympathy when I was stung by a bumble bee. I saw Nanny impatient in one moment and in the next lovingly kiss away the pain of a playground injury.

She didn't like people asking her a lot of questions. One day an inquisitive woman pointed out Nanny's fair complexion and asked her if she was Swedish. My Irish grandmother, in her best Swedish accent, replied, "Yaa." I was so stunned, I stopped breathing for a moment. That afternoon, Nanny and we kids giggled every time we thought about it or looked at each other. Some of the funniest times of my life were spent with Nanny. Wanting some peace and quiet, she once convinced those around her that she was asleep. Nanny shot me a wink. We laughed for hours!

Once I thought I heard Nanny talking to herself. I assumed that must be what older people do. Days later, I heard her whispered voice, "Father in Heaven, help me to..." At that moment I realized Nanny wasn't talking to herself, she was talking to God. Nanny was in constant prayer.

She taught me that no one and nothing is perfect here. We keep trying to do better, trust and persevere with God's help. We have faith that one day Jesus will "fix" us, just as He fixed the problem at the wedding feast.

PROCLAMATION OF THE KINGDOM

"Now after John was arrested, Jesus came into Galilee, preaching the gospel of God, and saying, 'The time is fulfilled, and the kingdom of God is at hand; repent and believe in the gospel.'"   Mark 1:14-15

"Repent." With God's grace I can reject sin and turn my heart to Jesus. I cannot do this without Him. He gives me the grace, and then I respond to His mercy and His love.

As I continue to fill my heart with Jesus, I can encourage my grandchildren to do the same. So long ago, my Nanny gestured quietly to me to sit near her while she prayed the Rosary. I heard her whispered "Our Fathers" and "Hail Marys." I heard her say each mystery and a small prayer with each one. It was peaceful and sweet. She was patient and gentle. I felt my heart longing and turning to God. The next day, when I noticed her reach into the pocket of her dress for her blue beads, I wondered if I would be invited to sit again. I was, and this time she handed me a small white Rosary. I didn't expect that, and I felt so loved. I watched and followed as she took hold of the crucifix and blessed herself. I did the same. I was nervous at the start of our very first Rosary together. I thought I might make mistakes reciting the Hail Mary or Our Father. Thankfully, Nanny did not require me to, but let me join in when I was ready.

Now I have precious moments with my grandchild. The first time Austin ran to me with outstretched arms yelling "Ah-ma!" he leaped into my arms and we both smiled, hugged and kissed one another. My heart was full as I realized I am just as important to him as he is to me.

I want to spend as much time with my grandchildren as possible, and with love and patience, encourage them to turn their hearts to God. I can pray Rosaries with them. We can visit Jesus in the Blessed Sacrament together. I can take them to Mass, and we can receive Holy Communion together. I can teach reverence to holy pictures and statues, our holy reminders. I can read the Bible to my grandchildren, pray with them and model the beauty of Confession. I can teach them, by example, to be charitable to others. If I do these things with a gentle heart, patience and great love, we will all grow closer to God.

4.

THE TRANSFIGURATION

"...He took with Him Peter and John and James, and went up on the mountain to pray. And as He was praying, the appearance of His countenance was altered, and His clothing became dazzling white...and they saw His glory...And a voice came out of the cloud, saying, 'This is my Son, my Chosen; listen to Him!'" Luke 9:28-29,32,35

Revealing our Lord's glory, the three disciples saw what was to come with His death and resurrection. When our earthly life is over, we have hope to live with Him in heaven for eternity, where there will be no pain or suffering. And there will be a day when our bodies also are glorified.

As after Jesus' baptism, God the Father again proclaimed Jesus' divinity: "This is my son, my chosen; listen to Him!" But how can we listen if we haven't set time aside to pray? How can we hear Jesus if we do not stop and quiet ourselves? Prayer is vital to a close relationship with God. Jesus and the Father are one, and you can't get any closer than that, and yet Jesus still prayed. How much more we need that time in prayer. If we become good listeners, we will hear amazing things.

There were many words that my grandparents spoke that I still hold dear. I listened to them. Taking their advice, I became more than I had been. Nanny told me to think about a career in nursing or teaching. When I started nursing school, she encouraged me with her heartening words, "You *can* become a nurse." I don't know how she knew I was doubting the possibility, but her faith in me gave me the courage to keep trying.

One morning before breakfast, she handed me a vial of insulin and a glass syringe and asked me to give her the morning injection. She had never gotten used to giving herself "diabetes shots." This was usually Foggy's duty, but I knew she was trying to give me an opportunity to learn. I was nervous, didn't want to hurt her and thus far had only practiced on oranges. She assured me it would be fine. So, Nanny received the first injection I ever gave to a person.

Though she didn't live with us, Nanny had a huge impact on my life, more than she probably ever knew. I was transformed by her love.

May we, as grandparents, always remember the power of our love and prayers to change things. Help us, Blessed Trinity, to be transformed by Your love and become a family ever more united in love, just like the Father, Son and Holy Spirit.

5.

THE INSTITUTION OF THE
HOLY EUCHARIST

"Jesus took bread, said the blessing, broke it and giving it to His disciples, said, 'Take and eat. This is my body.' Then He took a cup, gave thanks and gave it to them, saying, 'drink from it, all of you, for this is My blood of the Covenant, which will be shed on behalf of many for the forgiveness of sins.'"

Matthew 26:26-28

With perfect love, Jesus offered himself to God the Father as a sacrifice for our salvation. He still gives Himself to us perpetually in the Blessed Sacrament. All of Him is truly present: Body, Blood, Soul and Divinity.

As He gives completely of Himself, He calls each of us to give ourselves to each other. As grandparents we can "spend" ourselves — joyfully use up our earthly time, loving and helping.

I only have a few memories of my Grandpa John, as he died when I was young. But I remember very clearly that he once spent many hours trying to fix a toy for me. I was about three and remember handing it to him and checking on him every few minutes to see how he was doing. I can still hear Nana Roni laugh, and feel Grandpa John's dedication and love.

Jesus, You strengthen us with Your loving presence. We may grow weary. You refresh us. We may become focused on ourselves; You build us up to be more sacrificial. We may become impatient; You love us and give us the grace to be generous, gentle and kind.

You offer Yourself to us every day at Mass. You wait for us in the monstrance or the tabernacle. You wait to love us, nourish our souls and change us. All we need do is go humbly before You. You will change our hearts, our lives and our eternity.

Once while visiting our grandparents in New York City, we walked from Catholic church to Catholic church, stopping in each one to visit Jesus in the Blessed Sacrament and say a prayer. I will not forget the impact that had on me to this day as I came to understand the great gift of the Eucharist. I had already known that Jesus is present in Holy Communion, but I wrongly assumed He went back to heaven after Mass. Nanny explained that Jesus remains with us, and our journey from tabernacle to tabernacle revealed He is alive and with us here and on the next block simultaneously. As I imitated Nanny kneeling reverently, I felt Jesus' constant availability and incredible loving presence.

May I be able to pass on that same love for Jesus in the Blessed Sacrament to my grandchildren, so that they will hunger and thirst for Him. If I do nothing but that, I will have left a great legacy.

THE

SORROWFUL

MYSTERIES

1.

AGONY IN THE GARDEN

*"Jesus went with them to a place called Geth-
semane... Then He said to them, 'My soul is
very sorrowful, even to death; remain here and
watch with Me.'"*   Matthew 26:36,38

In a garden, Jesus continued His work
of salvation, restoring the paradise Adam lost
for the world in a garden that was meant to be
our eternal home with God. Adam and Eve
wanted to be the "gods" of what is good and
evil. They wanted to decide. God the Father
asked for obedience so that He could teach us
truth. It is not easy for us to discern truth
without God's guidance.

In His agony, Jesus faced what was
about to happen to Him on the cross. Feeling
the weight of the sins of the world and
abandoned by His friends, He suffered and
prayed so intently, His sweat became like
drops of blood.

Growing up on a farm, I thought of
Jesus in Gethsemane, while picking string
beans one hot summer morning. I was sweaty
and tired and would have rather been sitting
in front of a fan eating chocolate ice cream. I
knew that Jesus had suffered so much more,
but I couldn't help unite my little suffering to
His. Nanny taught me the concept of
spontaneous prayer. She sent up brief

messages to God throughout the day, opening up channels of His grace: "Father in Heaven, help us." "Thy will be done." "I offer this up."

My "agony" was very short lived. Some shade, a cool drink and I was ready for more work. As I watched my older brothers, Joey, Jimmy and John working in the fields, I felt proud. They looked so courageous and brave, grown-up heroes working for the good of us all. And I thought that was what Jesus did for us. He suffered for the good of us all.

We all have sufferings. It is part of this earthly life, since Adam and Eve's choice ushered sin and death into the world. Parents and grandparents have particular kinds of sufferings. I am not my grandchildren's parent. Perhaps I will not see them for an extended time or I will not have the kind of influence on their lives that I hope for and I will ache for them. Illness, pain, grieving or worry will make me suffer. In those moments, Jesus calls me to pray and unite my sufferings to His, just like I did in a much smaller way in the string bean field.

In the garden of Gethsemane, Jesus told His disciples, "Watch and pray." Elsewhere in Scripture, the Holy Spirit tells us to "Pray always." May we never forget the power of prayer to heal us and strengthen us in our sufferings.

2.

THE SCOURGING AT THE PILLAR

"Pilate said to them, 'Whom do you want me to release, Barabbas or Jesus?' He knew that it was out of envy that they had delivered Him up... And they said, 'Barabbas.' Pilate said, 'Then what shall I do with Jesus?' They all said, 'Let Him be crucified.' He said, 'Why, what evil has He done?' Then he released for them Barabbas, and having scourged Jesus, delivered Him to be crucified."

Matthew 27: 17-18, 21-23, 26

Pilate knew the chief priests and elders brought Jesus to him out of envy. They witnessed the people following Jesus and they saw Jesus as a threat to their power. The devil was also envious of God. He tempted Eve with his lies, leading her to envy what God possessed. Jesus came face to face with envy, continued to undo the errors of man's fall and saved us.

Pilate knew that Jesus was innocent, yet went along with the crowd and had Jesus scourged. The Roman governor was a coward. He didn't stand up for what he believed. The horrendous scourging was probably done using a Roman whip embedded with sharp pieces of lead used to remove pieces of flesh. Oh Jesus, how You suffered!

Nana Roni told me once that one of her sons had volunteered as a paratrooper in the

Army. One hot August day she received a telegram that he had been killed in the war. Family and friends gathered around her saying, "No, it can't be!" She was in agony hoping somehow there had been a mistake. (As I listened to Nana describe that horrible day, I held back my tears. I didn't want Nana to stop talking, and knew she would if she thought she upset me.) Later that week, Nana Roni received another telegram – her son was MIA, "Missing In Action." A final one delivered the message that he was WIA, "Wounded in Action." Thank God his whereabouts were known and he was alive! I knew all the while Nana was telling me that story that she was talking about my father, the man who had obviously survived the war, fallen in love, married my mother and was raising a family of eight children. But I was trying to put myself in Nana and Dad's places and imagine what they went through. They must have suffered so much. My heart ached for them. I just couldn't bear the pain they must have endured. I sometimes feel the same way when I contemplate Jesus' sufferings. Our Lord was so brave. My Dad was like Jesus in that way. He chose to enlist, to suffer for all. Jesus chose to suffer, to bring us everlasting life.

Sometimes living out our faith requires valor. May we all strive to live courageously. May Jesus give us strength to proclaim His word, suggest to our family we pray and use our time for God.

3.

THE CROWNING WITH THORNS

"Weaving a crown of thorns, they placed it on His head and a reed in His right hand. And kneeling before Him, they mocked Him, saying, 'Hail, King of the Jews!' They spat upon Him..."
Matthew 27:29-30

The soldiers inflicted horrible pain on our Lord's precious head. The thorns in the crown they wove were probably two inches long, sharp and broad. The pain and humiliation Jesus suffered was enormous, and yet He did not complain; He did not utter one word against His tormentors. He put Himself into the hands of the Father with complete confidence to endure the crown of thorns.

When I was young I heard the story of St. Maximilian Kolbe. Our Blessed Mother showed him two crowns. The white one was for purity and the red one was for martyrdom. She asked him which he would accept. He said both. I couldn't help but think of Nanny and Foggy. I used to imagine that they would be given crowns when they got to heaven because of the pain they had endured as children. Foggy's mother died when he was just two and Nanny's father died when she was seven.

They never shared this with me, but my mother did. It made me determined to be grateful for my family, and to never take my parents for granted. I could not think of a sadder story than a baby and a small child not having their mother and father, though I was sure their guardian angels and our Blessed Mother comforted them.

I also envisioned someday another crown would be waiting for my dad. Joseph DeMato was decorated with a Purple Heart after being wounded in Korea. When I first heard "He had a Purple Heart," I thought it was a disease. I was very upset. I finally got up the courage to approach my mom about my fears. She brought me to my dad, who showed me his amazing heart shaped medal. They smiled at my misinterpretation, and I was so relieved! I couldn't imagine my life without one of my parents, and yet I know Jesus would have been there for me, just as He was there for Nanny and Foggy, who grew closer to Him through their suffering.

Dear Jesus, King of Kings, You who should only be crowned with love, worship and adoration, strengthen us in all our trials! As we spend our time as a family knowing, loving and serving You, may You be adorned with the glory You deserve.

THE CARRYING OF THE CROSS

"And as they led Him away, they seized one Simon of Cyrene, who was coming in from the country, and laid on him the cross, to carry it behind Jesus."   Luke 23:26

By now, Jesus is bloodied and exhausted; tortured by rejection, envy, selfishness and hate. He can barely stand. The soldiers want someone to help Him carry the cross so that He does not die yet. In their cruelty, they want Him to get to Golgotha so He can be further tortured on the cross. None of His friends are there. They have all abandoned Him. There is no one to render aid to Him. So they make Simon, a stranger, His helper. We understand from this that Jesus will aid us in carrying our crosses. He will not abandon us.

When my mother was in the hospital with the birth of my precious brother, Danny, I missed her deeply. She was my life. I needed her kind, gentle presence every minute. I remember feeling so alone, so lost without Mommy. Nanny and Nana Roni took turns caring for us. Nanny would make chocolate pudding on the stove and kiss my cheeks nonstop. Nana Roni would kiss me, brush my hair and tell me it was curly like my daddy's. Nanny and Nana Roni cooked meals, washed the dishes, and loved us. They helped me carry a large cross and comforted me with the little things they did. I still remember the softest, most beautiful pink and yellow dresses Nana crocheted for my twin sisters and me. It was as though my grandparents were Jesus to me. I felt loved and protected.

Back then, my father said by the end of each day we were imitating our grandmothers. A few years ago, my daughter said she noticed when I pray the Rosary, I have an Irish brogue. I was surprised. Could it be that I became more like Nanny than I ever realized?

Jesus, You tell us to love others the way You loved us, sacrificially. Using our life to love, serve each other and make sacrifices undoes a multitude of sins. As I unite my sacrifices to Your suffering, to make up for my sins and the sins of the world, give me the grace to carry my crosses with patience and teach my grandchildren to do the same.

5.

THE CRUCIFIXION

"And when they had crucified Him... those who passed by derided Him, wagging their heads and saying, '...If You are the Son of God, come down off the cross.' So also the chief priests, with the scribes and elders mocked Him saying, 'He saved others; He cannot save himself.'"

Matthew 27:35,39,40-42

Along with physical suffering, Jesus also endured jeers and insults. The onlookers arrogantly taunted Him, bidding Him to come down from the cross to prove who He was. He did not respond, but let His silence speak. He persevered in His pain to fulfill the Father's plan of salvation.

He did not make it easy on Himself. The soldiers offered Him wine and gall, given as a narcotic to lessen pain, but He would not drink it. He was giving everything He had to give, feeling everything there was to feel.

He accepted the full brunt, for love of the Father and for releasing us from the bondage of sin and giving us eternal life. He suffered for all the sins of the world: past, present and future. He knew all; He knew that I would sin and He suffered so much for me. Jesus, I wish I could console You, especially for the pain I brought upon You.

Recently, I was holding my sixteen month old grandson, Austin. We were sharing an ice pop and smiling and laughing with each other. In turn, I tasted one side of the cool snack and he the other. It was a sweet moment loving each other, looking into each other's eyes and belonging to each other.

Austin said, "Ah-ma!" I said, "Yes, Austin?" He pointed to our crucifix on the wall. I said, "Do you want to say hi to Jesus?" Picking him up, I brought him over to Jesus on the cross.

Austin kissed Jesus and then moved my hand that was holding the ice pop, up to our Lord's mouth. He was giving Jesus a taste of refreshment. He was sharing our love with Jesus. I was overcome with emotion at the beautiful moment I was allowed to witness. Austin's love was there to console Jesus.

Holy Spirit, remind me, when I do good to others, I am consoling the body of Christ, His Church. Help me to take every opportunity to be kind, relieve suffering, and love others. Jesus, help me persevere to the end as You did!

THE

GLORIOUS

MYSTERIES

1.

THE RESURRECTION

"He is not here; for He has risen, as He said. Come, see the place where He lay. Then go quickly and tell His disciples that He has risen from the dead, and behold, He is going before You to Galilee; there You will see Him."

Matthew 28:6-7

Jesus, You live! What an amazing turn of events. When people thought You were at Your weakest, suffering a horrendous death, it was then that You were defeating death and sin! If ever we should doubt the possibility of new beginnings, we need only think of the empty tomb. "Behold, I make all things new," says the risen Lord. And He does it all for us. The Living God, the Good Shepherd saving us, loving us! He lays down His life for His sheep and then rises up to lead them to heaven.

When I was young and heard that "Jesus was the Good Shepherd," I dismissed it from my mind, thinking, "A Shepherd? Everyone knows St. Joseph taught Jesus to be a carpenter."

One day, while we walked around the farm, Foggy recited Psalm 23 to us children. He was so inspiring! And I loved him so much that everything he said became even more important. I reflected more deeply on "the Lord is my shepherd..." because I heard it from Foggy's own mouth.

I started to imagine myself as a little lamb being carried by Jesus. I was safe and secure in His strong arms. I imagined as we walked, Jesus whispered wonderful things about God the Father to me. He told me how much He loved me and how I could love Him. The longer I would see this image in my mind, the more I would become myself, the little child, in His arms. From that day on I saw Jesus in a new way. I had a new beginning with our Lord.

Now, my grandson is helping me see all things new. Recently, we adults sat down to dinner and began nibbling and talking before we said grace. Austin, not yet two years old, had his adorable hands folded in prayer. He looked at me and said, "Ah-ma!" He took one hand and touched his precious forehead and then his shoulder and back again to his forehead. We all got the message as this little cutie led us in prayer.

Jesus, You are the Resurrection and the Life. May we never forget that You are alive today with us in the Eucharist! In Holy Communion, we receive Your light, Your life, Your love. And we are blessed with a new beginning every time we receive You. May my entire life reflect a thanksgiving for that unfathomable gift. And may I encourage and inspire my grandchildren in their walk with the Good Shepherd, as my grandparents inspired me.

2.

THE ASCENSION

"Then He led them out as far as Bethany, and lifting up His hands He blessed them. While He blessed them, He parted from them, and was carried up into heaven."

Luke 24:50-51

Jesus, how could the men with You believe their own eyes? Watching You ascend into the sky toward heaven must have been utterly amazing! And yet I'm sure they wanted to call to You and beg You to stay forever or at least for a little longer. I'm sure they missed You instantly.

When we lived on Long Island, Nanny and Foggy usually visited for three or four days at a time. Watching them pack their car to get ready to go back to the city, we would feel miserable. After kisses and hugs, Nanny would roll down her window of their black Ford as Foggy circled the drive. She would poke her hand out and begin waving goodbye. Chasing their car for a number of yards, we kids must have looked like the Munchkins in the *Wizard of Oz*, running and yelling goodbye to Glinda. As my grandparents reached the fork in the road, Nanny would extend her entire arm out the window, continuing her enthusiastic wave. We watched the car enter the main road and fade from sight. A tear in my mother's eye signified the visit was officially over.

I used to imagine they were calling out to us too, saying, "be good" or "listen to Your Mom and Dad" or "don't fight with each other." It would seem like forever before we could see them again. I used to secretly pray that they would move in with us. I wanted to keep them always very close. Life was just so right when they were there.

I still miss them so. But I know they are still with us. St. John Chrysostom said about Jesus, "He whom we love and lose is no longer where He was before; He is now wherever we are." Just as Jesus became closer to us after His ascension, so too, my dad and grandparents are even closer to me now. They live right here in my heart.

3

THE DESCENT OF THE HOLY SPIRIT

"When the day of Pentecost had come, they were all together in one place. And suddenly a sound came from heaven like the rush of a mighty wind...And they were all filled with the Holy Spirit..."

(Acts 2:1-2,4)

Being filled with the Holy Spirit, the disciples each received an outpouring of grace and a new beginning. I pray that the Holy Spirit will renew me daily. I want to take my newness and use it for others. I want to be open to the Holy Spirit, be ready for anything and do what He is asking me to do.

Recently I made a "wrong" turn, while driving to visit my daughter and grandson. As in the past, I could have been annoyed by the inconvenience I just caused myself. But that day I was praying to the Holy Spirit to help me to be open to His will. So I continued on that path and said, "Lord, perhaps You want me on this road." A few minutes later, I spotted someone on the side of the road with a broken-down car and tow truck.

As I got closer, I realized it was my friend, Maria. I parked and began to walk toward her, calling her name. Looking in the direction of my voice, she raised her hand to shield the sun from her eyes. As I got closer she said, "Oh Anne, it's you! With the sun behind your head, you looked like the angel I was praying for! The tow truck will take my car to the shop, but I need to get these groceries home. My cell phone died. I didn't know how I was going to get home."

The Holy Spirit had answered both of our prayers, and I was happy to share the story with my daughter when I finally reached her house and got my hugs and kisses from my precious grandson. We marveled at how our awesome God leads us to where He wants us to be. May we always listen to His promptings.

Come Holy Ghost, Creator blest. And in our hearts take up Thy rest. Come with Thy grace and heavenly aide, to fill the hearts which Thou hast made. Nanny and I quietly sang that song in the living room once while everyone else was making all kinds of noise in the kitchen. We giggled at the fact that none of them knew.

Holy Spirit, come, fill my heart!

4.

THE ASSUMPTION

"Therefore my heart is glad and my soul rejoices, my body, too, abides in confidence; Because You will not abandon my soul to the nether world, nor will You suffer Your faithful one to undergo corruption."

Psalms 16:9-10

Jesus, when our Blessed Mother's earthly life was over, You exalted her above all the angels and saints, bringing her "body and soul" to heaven with You. Although the disciples would have been saddened by her absence, they also must have marveled at her amazing, happy death. She, who was given to us as our Mother, continues this love in her heavenly Motherhood.

As a child, this was my favorite mystery because the Assumption of the Blessed Virgin Mary was the name of our church. It also celebrated my love for Mary and the hope that we, too, would go to heaven for eternity. Although I never asked her, I thought this was Nanny's favorite mystery too. She told me Our Blessed Mother is the most humble person there will ever be. She explained that humility is the hardest virtue to attain. I loved talking to Nanny as she shared her wisdom with me: "Get plenty of sunshine!" and "Don't make your life so hectic that you don't have time to think about Holy God."

On a bright, breezy fall day, Nanny and I sat on our aluminum folding chairs while my adorable baby sister, JoEllen, romped in her wooden play yard. She called to me, and I immediately jumped up to get her. Nanny said, "Oh, Annie will spoil that wee one. The baby of the family is always spoiled." I turned and said, "Oh, I'm sorry Nanny." Then I paused, felt confused and asked timidly, "But Nanny, aren't *you* the youngest in *your* family?" She smiled, then chuckled and said, "Oh no, I am not spoiled, I am very humble and always patient." She began to laugh, and so did I. I knew that Nanny wasn't always patient, but here I saw that she knew it too. And I enjoyed her wonderful laugh as she playfully teased herself.

Blessed Mother, teach me joyfulness in humility!

5.

THE CORONATION

"A great sign appeared in the sky, a woman clothed with the sun, with the moon under her feet, and on her head a crown of twelve stars." Revelation 12:1

As the Blessed Trinity honors Mary, so do we. God the Father gave Mary the unique honor of being the new Ark of the Covenant, the one who would bear Jesus. The Holy Spirit anointed her and honored her. Through His power, she is the Mother of God. Jesus honored and obeyed her. His love protected her and consoled her even through His suffering and death. All of heaven rejoiced when she was crowned queen.

Strong devotion to Mary brings us closer to Jesus. Our love for her only magnifies our love for God. When we give her our prayers and good deeds, she takes them and makes them so much more precious. Then she gives them to Jesus for us, multiplied and wrapped in her beauty.

We approach her loveliness to learn from her perfect humility, sweetness, purity, patience, obedience, continual prayer, self-denial, wisdom, faith and love of God.

Nanny shared with me the beautiful and close relationship she had with Jesus' Mother. "Lena" (Kathleen) Duffy, changed her name to Katherine when she arrived at Ellis Island from Ireland at age eighteen. The boat trip had been long and grueling. Praying the Rosary during their journey, she felt such peace and comfort. Nanny said when she first spotted Lady Liberty, the grand statue in the sea, she looked like our Blessed Mother welcoming her. Nanny knew that she would love her new country and was so grateful to God for the safe trip and the new life that lay ahead. And indeed, the future held many blessings, including a fifty-six-year marriage, five children, twenty-five grandchildren, forty-six great-grandchildren and twelve great-great-grandchildren.

Holy Mother of God, pray for my seven brothers and sisters and their families, my husband's family, our parents, grandparents, aunts, uncles and cousins, our children and our children's children.

Already, I can see the fruit of Your love in my little grandchild. When Austin sees the statue of Our Lady of Guadalupe, he grabs my hand exclaiming, "Guada-Guada!" With his other precious hand, he presents her with a backyard treasure — a perfect green leaf or a beautiful shiny rock, laying it gently at her feet.

Indeed, Blessed Mother, all generations call You blessed! Exalted by Jesus as Queen of heaven and earth, Dear Mother of God, Mother of Mercy, Mother of us all, pray for us!

HOW TO PRAY THE ROSARY

1. While holding the crucifix, make the SIGN OF THE CROSS: "In the name of the Father, and of the Son and of the Holy Spirit. Amen."

2. Then, recite the APOSTLE'S CREED:
"I BELIEVE IN GOD, the Father almighty, Creator of heaven and earth, and in Jesus Christ, His only Son, our Lord, who was conceived by the Holy Spirit, born of the Virgin Mary, suffered under Pontius Pilate, was crucified, died and was buried; He descended into hell; on the third day He rose again from the dead; He ascended into heaven, and is seated at the right hand of God the Father almighty; from there He will come to judge the living and the dead. I believe in the Holy Spirit, the Holy Catholic Church, the communion of saints, the forgiveness of sins, the resurrection of the body, and life everlasting. Amen."

3. Recite the OUR FATHER on the first large bead:
"OUR FATHER, Who art in heaven, Hallowed be Thy Name. Thy Kingdom come. Thy Will be done, on earth as it is in Heaven. Give us this day our daily bread. And forgive us our trespasses, as we forgive

those who trespass against us. And lead us not into temptation, but deliver us from evil. Amen."

4. On each of the three small beads, recite a HAIL MARY for the increase of faith, hope and love. "HAIL MARY, full of grace, the Lord is with thee; Blessed art thou among women, and blessed is the fruit of thy womb, Jesus. Holy Mary, Mother of God, pray for us sinners, now and at the hour of death. Amen."

5. Recite the GLORY BE on the next large bead.
"GLORY BE to the Father, and to the Son, and to the Holy Spirit. As it was in the beginning, is now, and ever shall be, world without end. Amen."

6. Recall the first Rosary mystery and recite the Our Father on the next large bead.

7. On each of the adjacent ten small beads (known as a decade,) recite a Hail Mary while reflecting on the mystery.

8. On the next large bead, recite the Glory Be.

9. The FATIMA PRAYER may be said here:

"O MY JESUS, forgive us our sins, save us from the fires of hell, lead all souls to heaven, especially those who are in most need of Thy mercy."

10. Begin the next decade by recalling the next mystery and reciting an Our Father. Move to the small beads and pray ten Hail Marys while meditating on the mystery.

11. Continue until you have circled the entire Rosary (five decades.) Or for a full Rosary, you will circle it four times (twenty decades.)

12. It is customary to CONCLUDE with the following prayers:

HAIL HOLY QUEEN

"HAIL, HOLY QUEEN, mother of mercy, our life, our sweetness, and our hope. To thee do we cry, poor banished children of Eve. To thee do we send up our sighs, mourning and weeping in this valley of tears. Turn then, most gracious advocate, thine eyes of mercy toward us, and after this our exile, show us the blessed fruit of thy womb, Jesus. O clement, O loving, O sweet Virgin Mary.
(Verse) Pray for us, O Holy Mother of God.

(Response) That we may be made worthy of the promises of Christ."

ROSARY PRAYER

(Verse) Let us pray,
(Response) O God, whose only begotten Son, by His life, death, and resurrection, has purchased for us the rewards of eternal salvation, grant, we beseech Thee, that while meditating on these mysteries of the most holy Rosary of the Blessed Virgin Mary, that we may both imitate what they contain and obtain what they promise, through Christ our Lord. Amen.

Most Sacred Heart of Jesus, have mercy on us.

Immaculate Heart of Mary, pray for us.

In the Name of the Father, and of the Son and of the Holy Spirit. Amen.

WING TIP
by Sherry Boas

Dante De Luz's steel was forged in his youth, in the crucible of harsh losses and triumphant love. But that steel gets tested like never before as the revelation of a family secret presents the young Catholic priest with the toughest challenge of his life, with stakes that couldn't get any higher.

ROSARY TITLES AVAILABLE FROM CARITAS PRESS / CATHOLIC WORD

A Mother's Bouquet
Rosary Meditations for Moms

A Father's Heart
Rosary Meditations for Dads

A Child's Treasure
Rosary Meditations for Children

Amazing Love
Rosary Meditations for Teens

Generations of Love
Rosary Meditations for Grandparents

A Servant's Heart
Rosary Meditations for Altar Servers

Visit www.LilyTrilogy.com

www.LilyTrilogy.com

Caritas Press

(602) 920-2846

Email: Sherry@LilyTrilogy.com

Made in the USA
Columbia, SC
22 October 2023